RECORDED VERSIONS GUITAR

AUTHENTIC TRANSCRIPTIONS
WITH NOTES AND TABLATURE

**Transcribed by
JESSE GRESS**

STEVIE RAY VAU...
IN THE BEGINNING

T0045112

Notation Legend

Photos: Daniel Schaefer
ISBN 0-7935-2275-7

Hal Leonard Publishing Corporation

7777 West Bluemound Road P.O. Box 13819 Milwaukee, WI 53213

In The Open

Words and Music by Sonny Thompson and Freddie King

* Parenthesized chord symbols outline
  overall harmony.

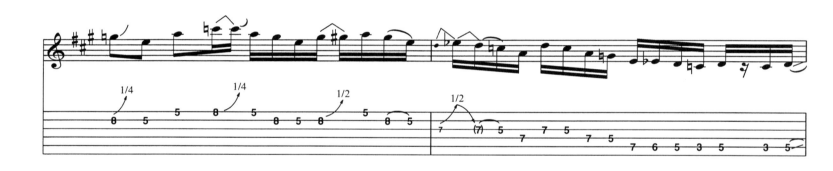

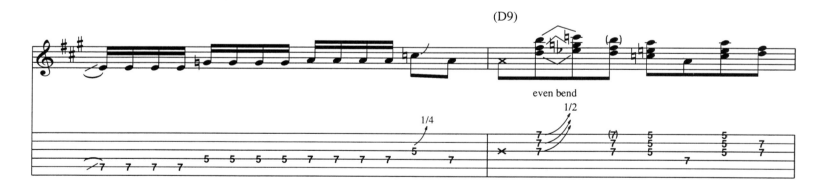

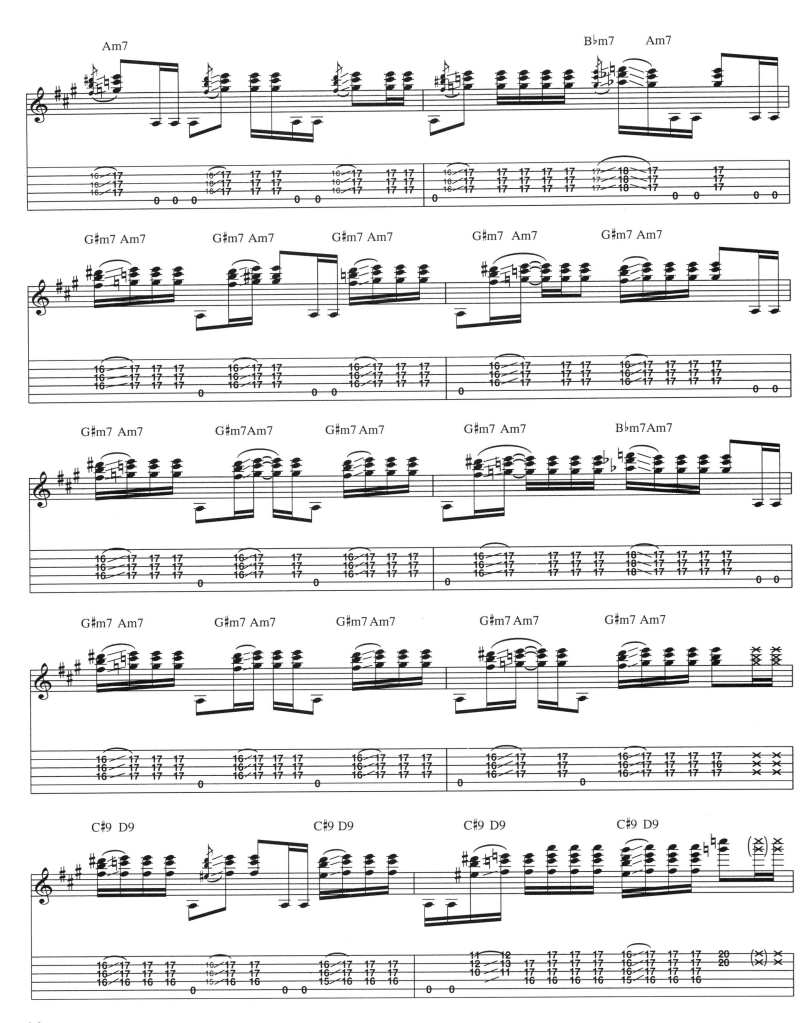

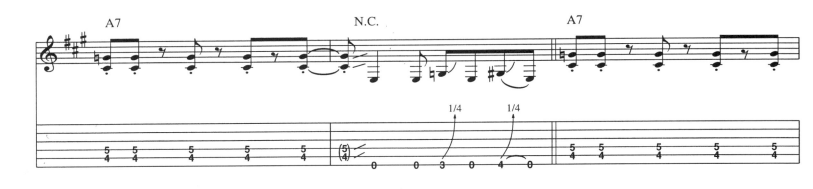

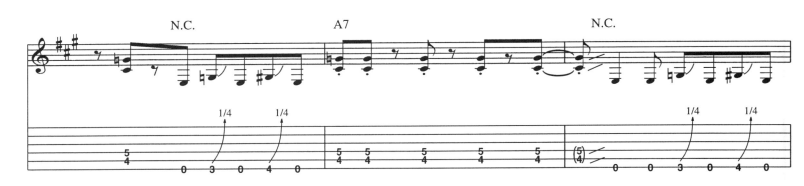

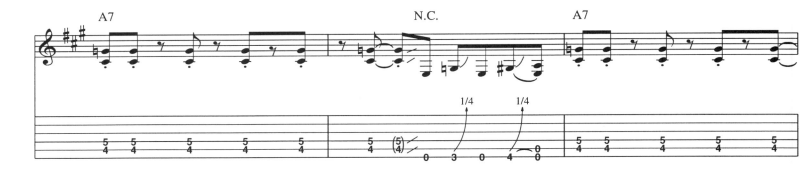

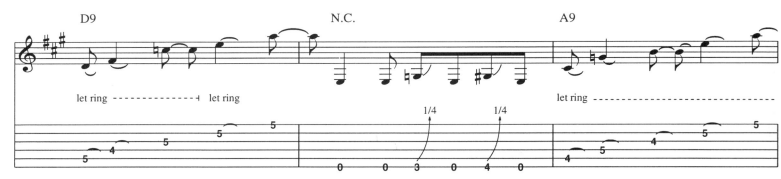

Slide Thing

Words and Music by Stevie Ray Vaughan

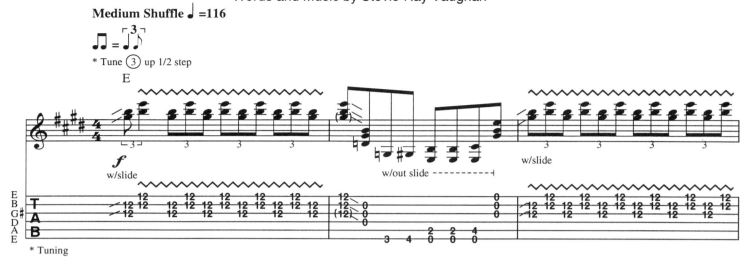

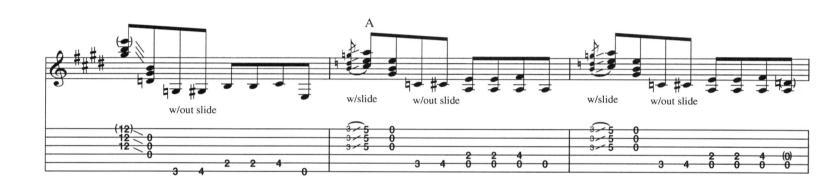

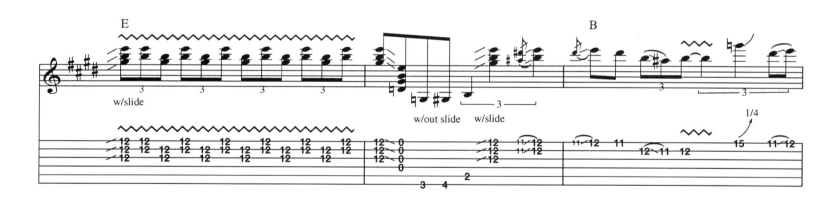

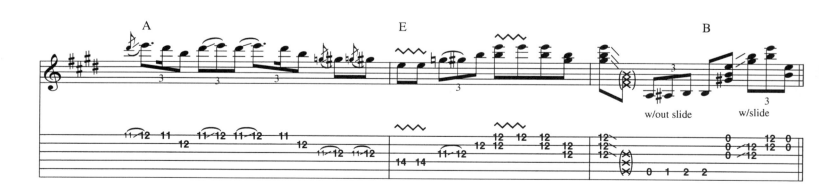

24

They Call Me Guitar Hurricane

(a.k.a. They Call Me Guitar Slim)

Written By Eddie "Guitar Slim" Jones

* Chord symbols outline
overall harmony

MCA music publishing

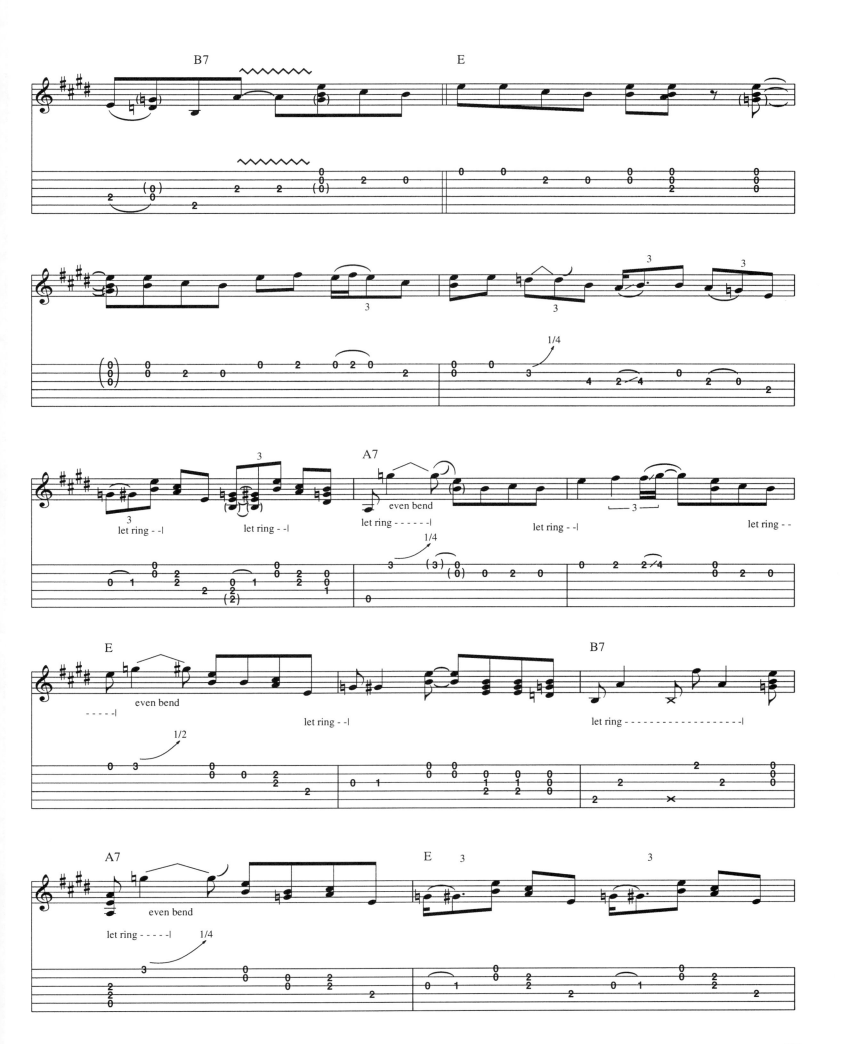

I'll drop ___ your town. ___

Outro chorus

All Your Love (I Miss Loving)

Words and Music by Otis Rush

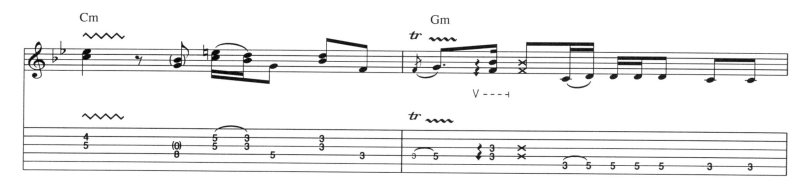

1st Verse

2nd Verse

2. All your love _____ pret - ty ba - by,   I have in store for you. __

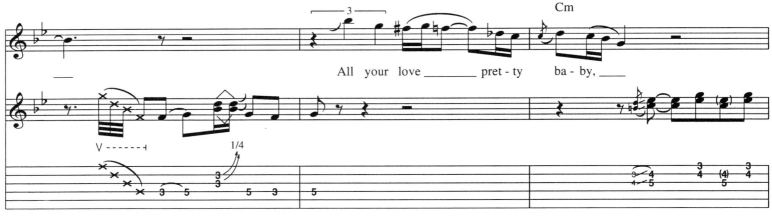

___   All your love _____ pret - ty ba - by, ____

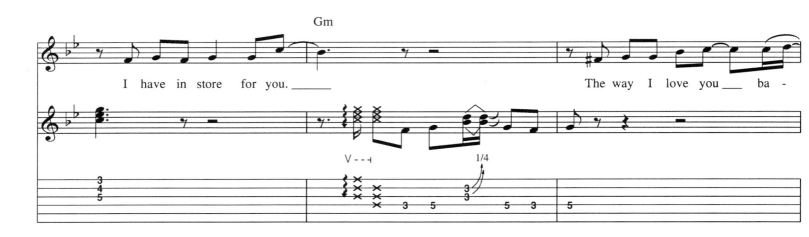

I have in store for you. _____   The way I love you ___ ba -

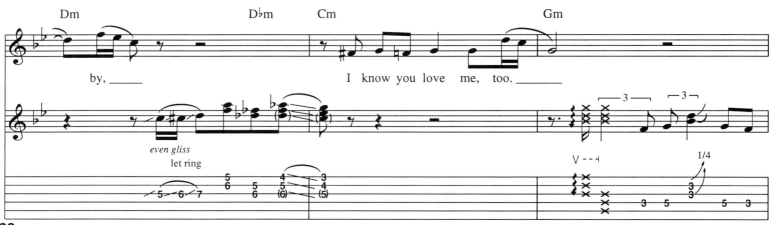

by, _____   I know you love me, too. _____

even gliss
let ring

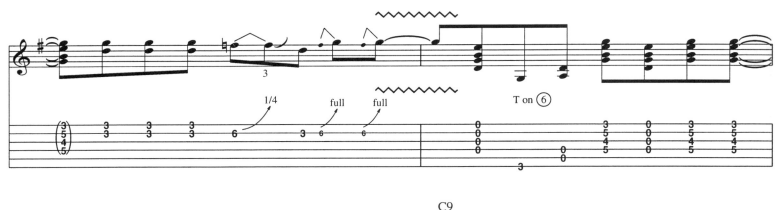

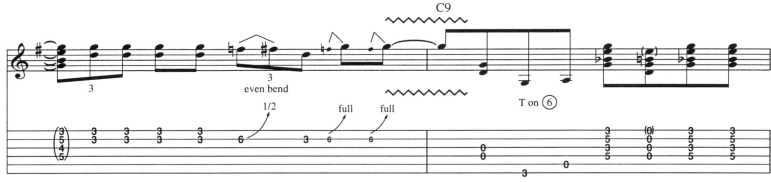

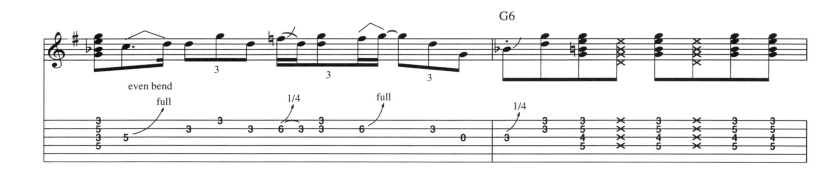

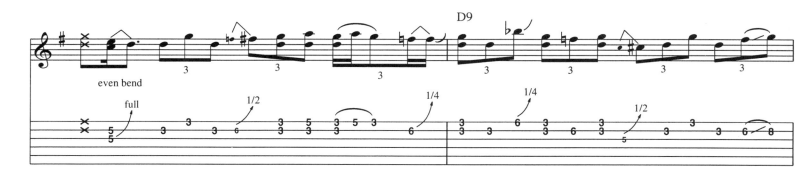

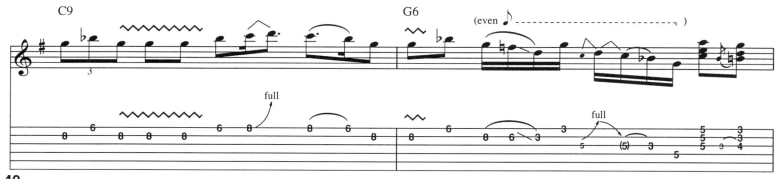

40

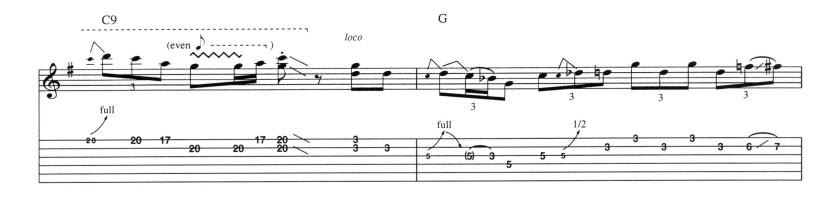

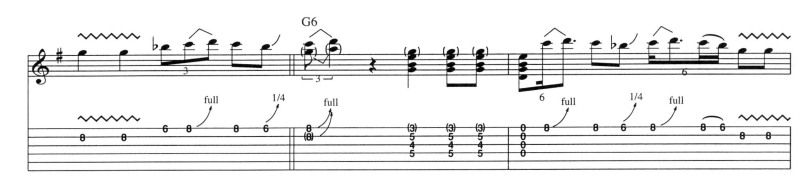

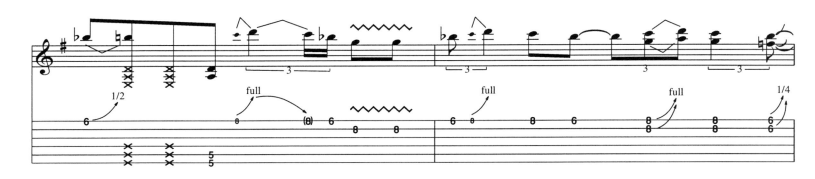

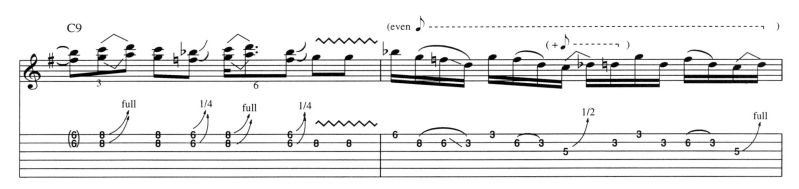

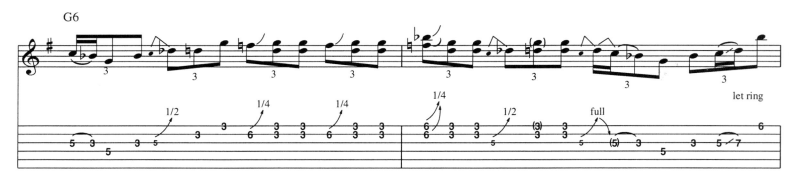

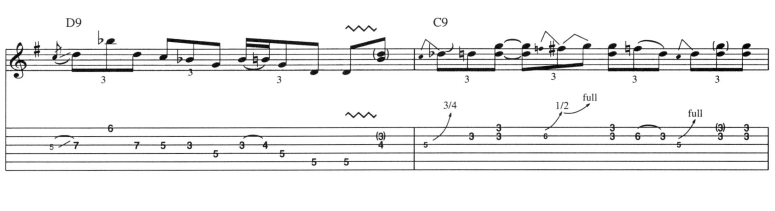

3rd Verse

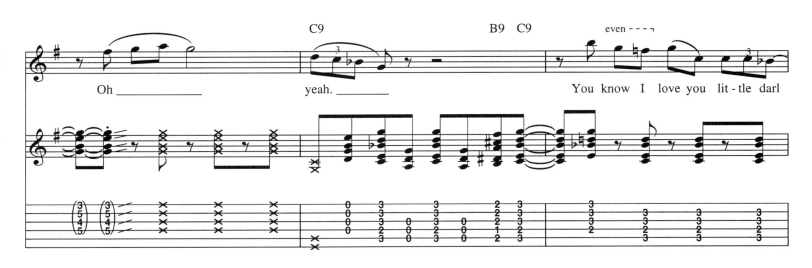

I know you love me, too. _____

Guitar solo 2

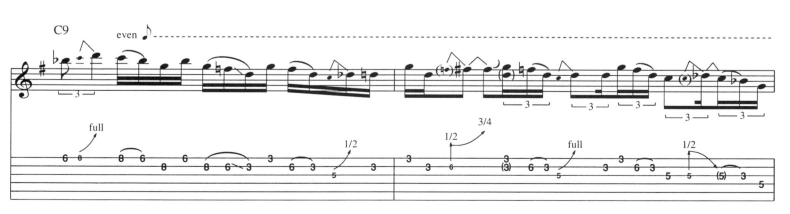

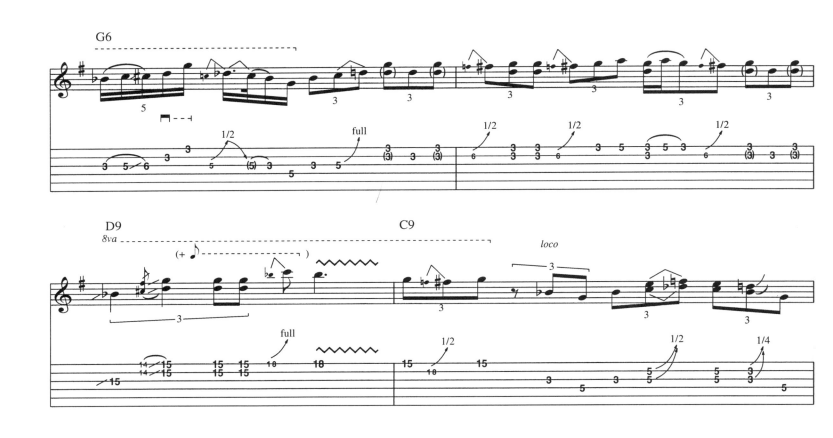

7th Verse

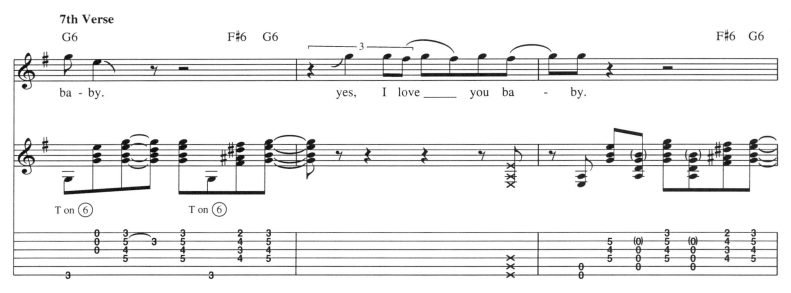

50

Tin Pan Alley

Words and Music by Robert Geddins

Slow Blues ♩ = 51

* Chord symbols outline overall harmony.

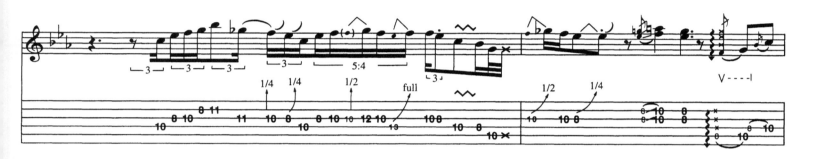

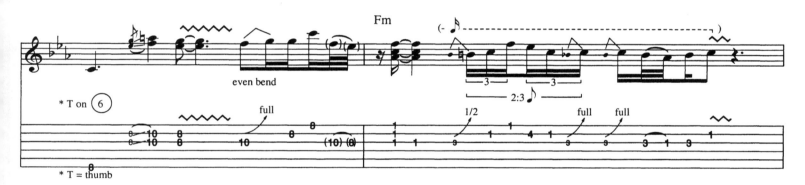

* T on ⑥

* T = thumb

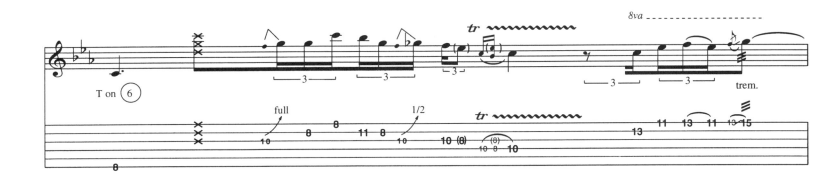

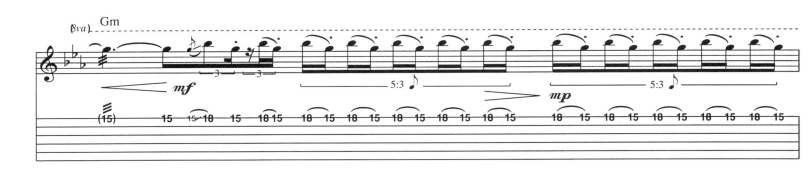

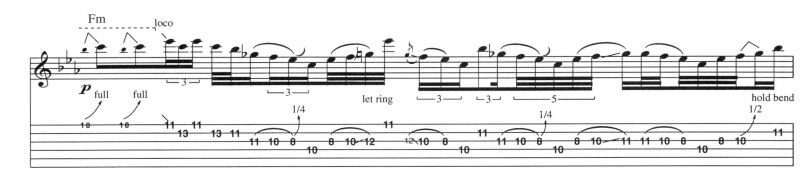

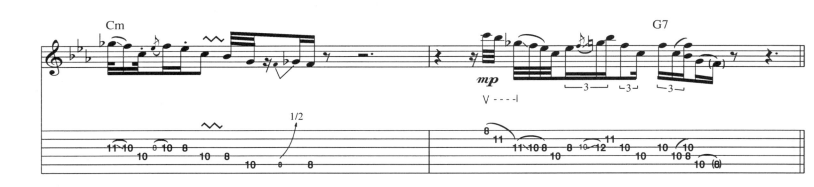

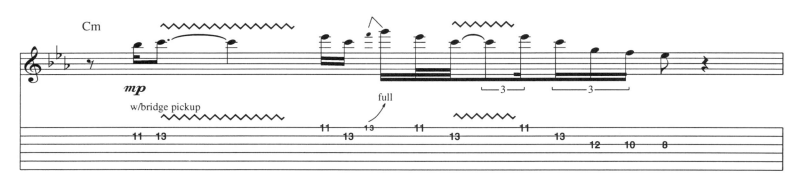

1. Went down to Tin Pan Al- ley, see what was go- in' on.

Lord, _ with a two - by - four. __ Hey, _____

al - ley's the rough - est place I've ev - er been. _____

All the peo- ple down there _

liv - in' for their whis - key, wine 'n' gin. _____

3rd Verse

3. I heard a pis-tol shoot, it ah was a for-ty-four. _____

Some-bod-y killed a crap shoot-er 'cause he did-n't

shake, rat-tle `n' roll. Hey, _____

al - ley's the rough - est place I've ev-er been. _____

All the peo-ple down there _____

can't af-ford their whis - key, wine 'n' gin. _____

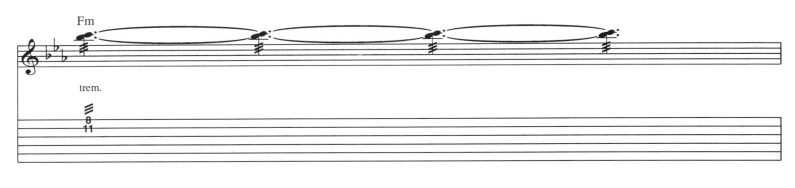

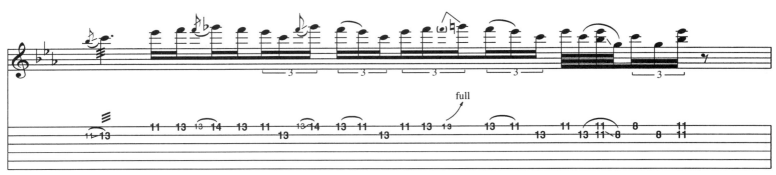

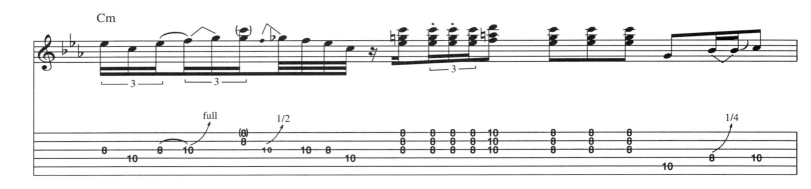

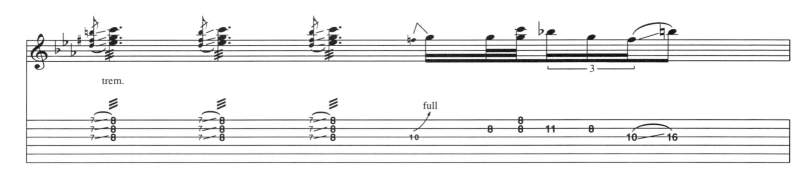

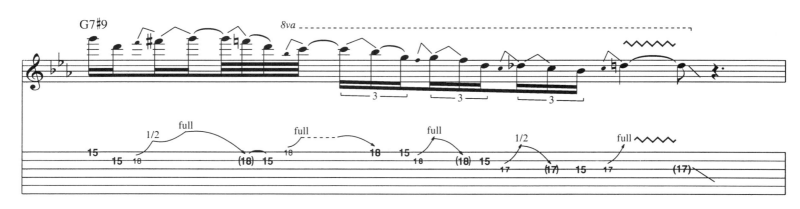

4th Verse

I saw a cop stand-in' _ with his hand on his gun. _____

Said "This is a raid, boy, no - bod-y run!" _ Hey, _____

al- ley's the rough- est place I've ev-er been. _____

an' took me right on to the bend. _____

Love Struck Baby

Words and Music by Stevie Ray Vaughan

* Chord symbols outline overall harmony.

threw a ton of bricks that hit me in the head ___ an' what cha do ___ lit - tle ba - by ain't

o - ver it yet. Ev - 'ry time I see ya make me feel so fine, ____ my

heart beats craz - y, my blood's ___ a run - nin' wild. Lov - in' make me feel ____ like a -

might - y, might - y fine. __ Love _____ me, mm - ba - by, I know _____ you're mine. __ I'm a

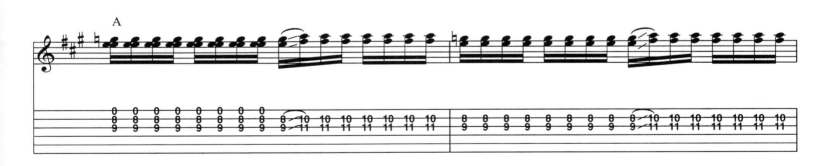

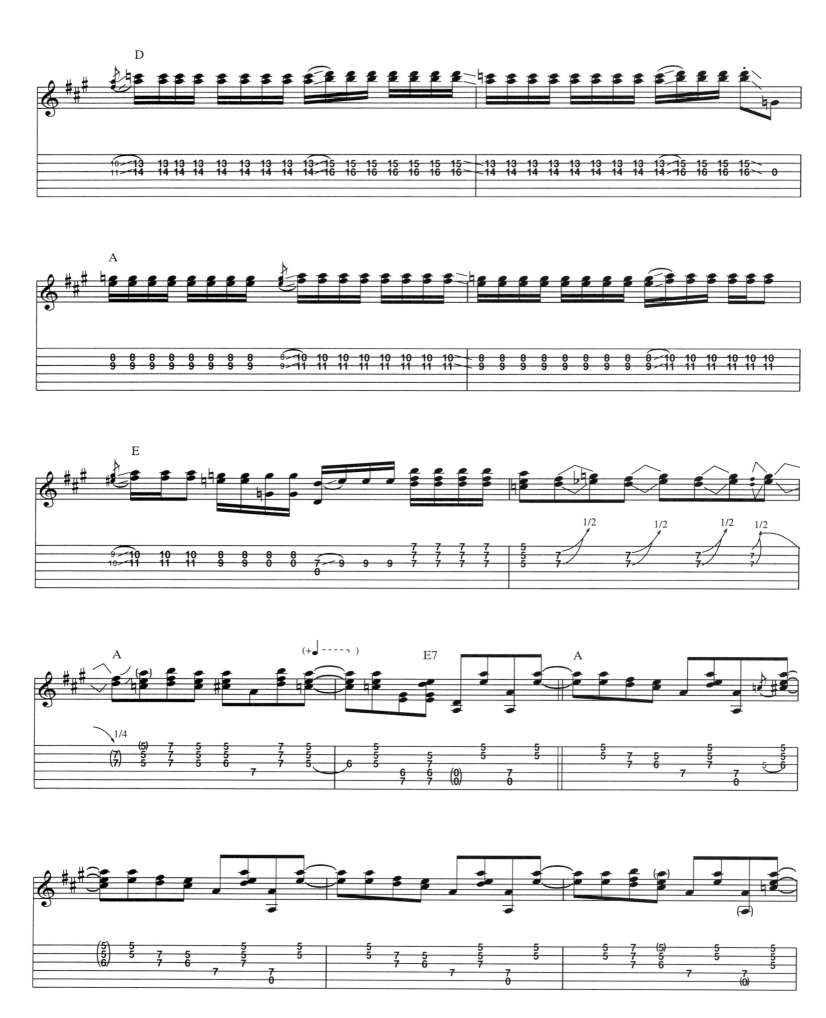

77

Chorus

Tell Me

Words and Music by Chester Burnett (a.k.a. Howlin' Wolf)

* Chord symbols outline overall harmony

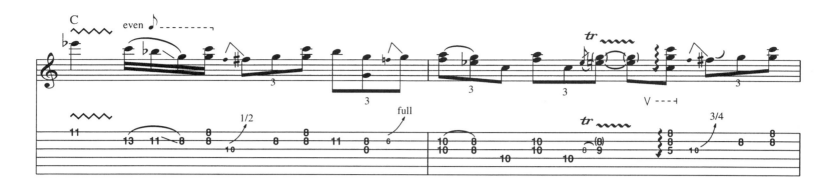

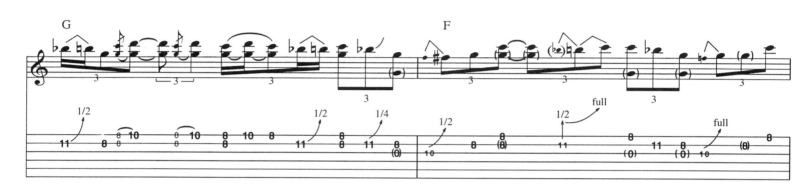

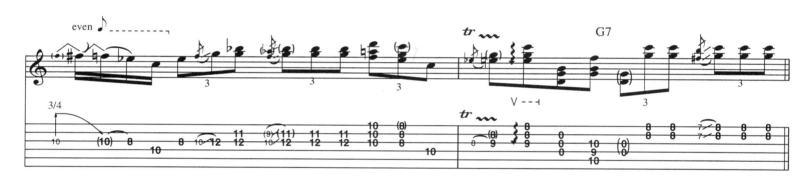

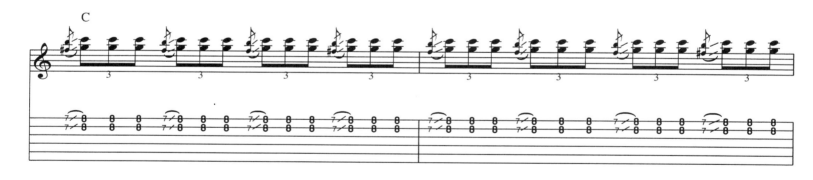

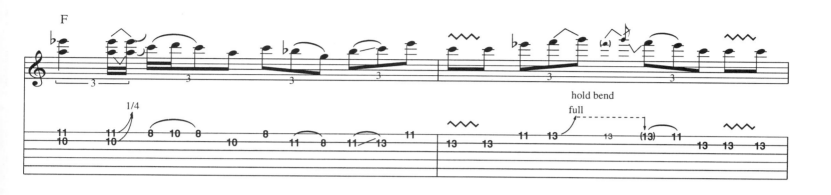

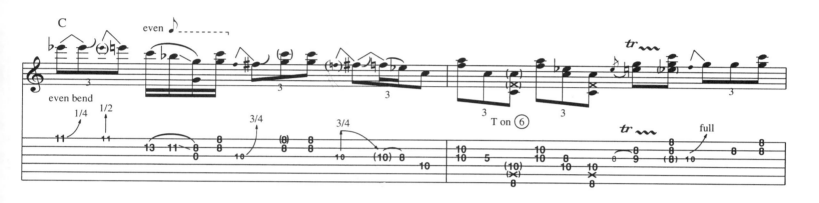

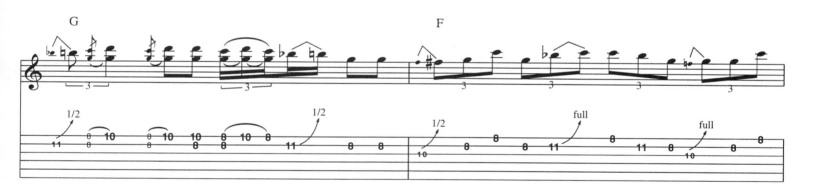

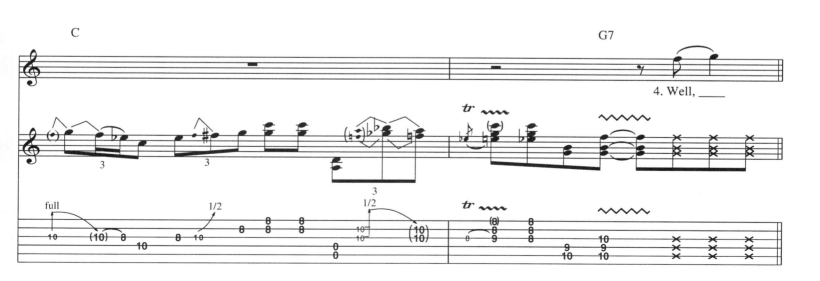

Shake For Me

Written by Willie Dixon

2nd Verse

went a - way ba - by,   you got back a lit - tle too late. ___

You ___

went a - way ba - by,   you got back a lit - tle too late. ___

I got a

shake __ it lit-tle ba - by, shake it for ____ me.

Yeah, now

shake lit-tle ba - by, shake it for ___ me.

Yeah. now

shake.　　　　　　　　　　　　　　　　　　　　　　Now let it

shake.　　　　　　　　　　　　　　　　　　　　　　Let it

shake a lit - tle ba - by,　　　shake like a wil - low tree.

Live Another Day

Words and Music by Stevie Ray Vaughan

*Chord symbols outline overall harmony

Sit - tin' here so lone - ly, tears keep fall - in' just like rain, _____ so I'm cry -

- 'in'.   Why'd I have _____ to feel _____ this

way _____ ah?   (If) I

can't   love   my   ba - by,   I   can't ah live an - oth - er   day __

3rd Verse

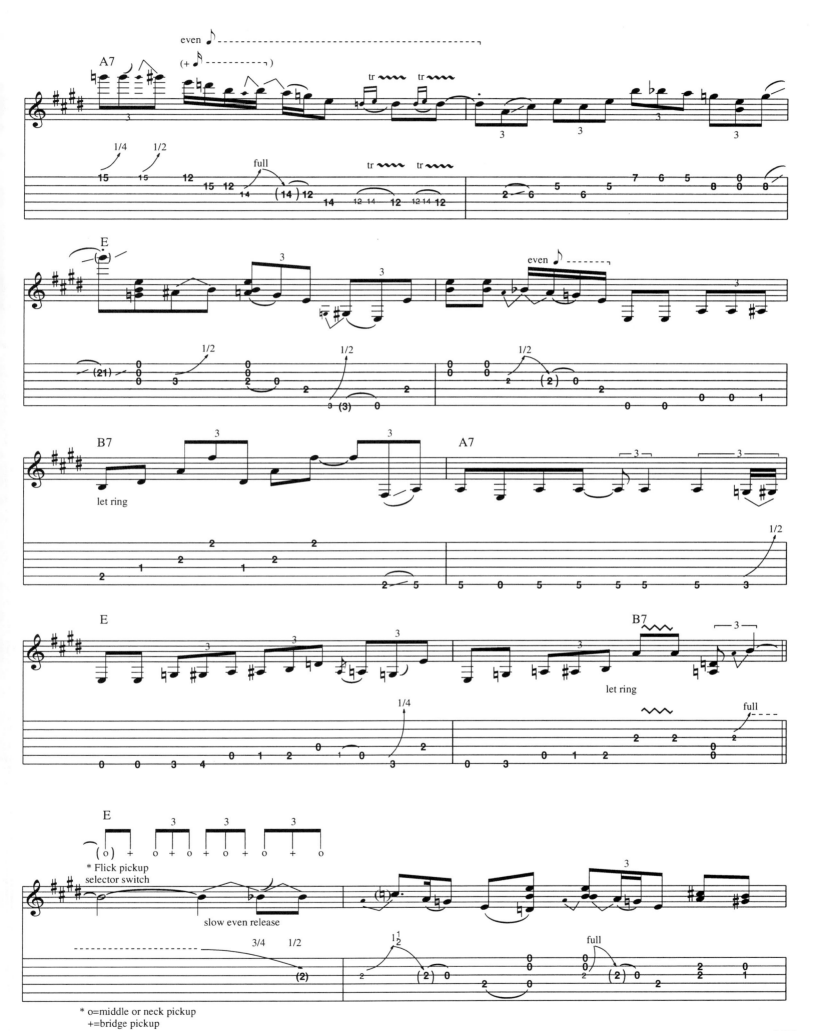

108

4th Verse

Yeah, _____ when I first met you ba - by,

things seemed to be fine. But now when we're to-geth-er, yeah,____ it's a

to-tal waste of time,____ so I'm cryin',___

Why ____ do I have ___ to feel this way ____ yeah?

If I can't love my ba-by,